Myth and Romance

Madison Cawein

Contents

MYTH AND ROMANCE

BY

Madison Cawein

TO
MY FRIEND
WILLIAM WARWICK THUM

PROEM.

There is no rhyme that is half so sweet
As the song of the wind in the rippling wheat;
There is no metre that's half so fine
As the lilt of the brook under rock and vine;
And the loveliest lyric I ever heard
Was the wildwood strain of a forest bird.--
If the wind and the brook and the bird would teach
My heart their beautiful parts of speech.
And the natural art that they say these with,
My soul would sing of beauty and myth
In a rhyme and a metre that none before
Have sung in their love, or dreamed in their lore,
And the world would be richer one poet the more.

VISIONS AND VOICES

Myth and Romance

I

When I go forth to greet the glad-faced Spring,
  Just at the time of opening apple-buds,
When brooks are laughing, winds are whispering,
  On babbling hillsides or in warbling woods,
  There is an unseen presence that eludes:--
Perhaps a Dryad, in whose tresses cling
  The loamy odors of old solitudes,
Who, from her beechen doorway, calls; and leads
  My soul to follow; now with dimpling words
  Of leaves; and now with syllables of birds;
While here and there--is it her limbs that swing?
Or restless sunlight on the moss and weeds?

II

Or, haply, 't is a Naiad now who slips,
  Like some white lily, from her fountain's glass,
While from her dripping hair and breasts and hips,
  The moisture rains cool music on the grass.
  Her have I heard and followed, yet, alas!
Have seen no more than the wet ray that dips
  The shivered waters, wrinkling where I pass;
But, in the liquid light, where she doth hide,
  I have beheld the azure of her gaze
  Smiling; and, where the orbing ripple plays,
Among her minnows I have heard her lips,
Bubbling, make merry by the waterside.

III

Or now it is an Oread--whose eyes
  Are constellated dusk--who stands confessed,
As naked as a flow'r; her heart's surprise,
  Like morning's rose, mantling her brow and breast:
  She, shrinking from my presence, all distressed
Stands for a startled moment ere she flies,
  Her deep hair blowing, up the mountain crest,
Wild as a mist that trails along the dawn.
  And is't her footfalls lure me? or the sound
  Of airs that stir the crisp leaf on the ground?
And is't her body glimmers on yon rise?
Or dog-wood blossoms snowing on the lawn?

IV

Now't is a Satyr piping serenades
  On a slim reed. Now Pan and Faun advance
Beneath green-hollowed roofs of forest glades,
  Their feet gone mad with music: now, perchance,
  Sylvanus sleeping, on whose leafy trance
The Nymphs stand gazing in dim ambuscades
  Of sun-embodied perfume.--Myth, Romance,
Where'er I turn, reach out bewildering arms,
  Compelling me to follow. Day and night
  I hear their voices and behold the light
Of their divinity that still evades,
And still allures me in a thousand forms.

Genius
Loci

I

What wood-god, on this water's mossy curb,
  Lost in reflections of earth's loveliness,
Did I, just now, unconsciously disturb?
  I, who haphazard, wandering at a guess,
Came on this spot, wherein, with gold and flame
Of buds and blooms, the season writes its name.--
Ah, me! could I have seen him ere alarm

Of my approach aroused him from his calm!
  As he, part Hamadryad and, mayhap,
Part Faun, lay here; who left the shadow warm
  As wildwood rose, and filled the air with balm
  Of his sweet breath as with ethereal sap.

II

Does not the moss retain some vague impress,
  Green dented in, of where he lay or trod?
Do not the flow'rs, so reticent, confess
  With conscious looks the contact of a god?
Does not the very water garrulously
Boast the indulgence of a deity?
And, hark! in burly beech and sycamore
  How all the birds proclaim it! and the leaves
  Rejoice with clappings of their myriad hands!
And shall not I believe, too, and adore,
  With such wide proof?--Yea, though my soul perceives
  No evident presence, still it understands.

III

And for a while it moves me to lie down
  Here on the spot his god-head sanctified:
Mayhap some dream he dreamed may lingert brown
  And young as joy, around the forestside;
Some dream within whose heart lives no disdain
For such as I whose love is sweet and sane;

That may repeat, so none but I may hear--
  As one might tell a pearl-strung rosary--
  Some epic that the trees have learned to croon,
Some lyric whispered in the wild-flower's ear,
  Whose murmurous lines are sung by bird and bee,
  And all the insects of the night and noon.

IV

For, all around me, upon field and hill,
  Enchantment lies as of mysterious flutes;
As if the music of a god's good-will
  Had taken on material attributes
In blooms, like chords; and in the water-gleam,
That runs its silvery scales from stream to stream;
In sunbeam bars, up which the butterfly,
  A golden note, vibrates then flutters on--
  Inaudible tunes, blown on the pipes of Pan,
That have assumed a visible entity,
  And drugged the air with beauty so, a Faun,
  Behold, I seem, and am no more a man.

The
Rain-Crow

I

Can freckled August,--drowsing warm and blonde
  Beside a wheat-shock in the white-topped mead,
In her hot hair the oxeyed daisies wound,--
  O bird of rain, lend aught but sleepy heed
  To thee? when no plumed weed, no feather'd seed
Blows by her; and no ripple breaks the pond,
  That gleams like flint between its rim of grasses,
  Through which the dragonfly forever passes
      Like splintered diamond.

II

Drouth weights the trees, and from the farmhouse eaves
  The locust, pulse-beat of the summer day,
Throbs; and the lane, that shambles under leaves
  Limp with the heat--a league of rutty way--
  Is lost in dust; and sultry scents of hay
Breathe from the panting meadows heaped with sheaves--
  Now, now, O bird, what hint is there of rain,
  In thirsty heaven or on burning plain,
      That thy keen eye perceives?

III

But thou art right. Thou prophesiest true.
  For hardly hast thou ceased thy forecasting,
When, up the western fierceness of scorched blue,
  Great water-carrier winds their buckets bring
  Brimming with freshness. How their dippers ring
And flash and rumble! lavishing dark dew
  On corn and forestland, that, streaming wet,
  Their hilly backs against the downpour set,
        Like giants vague in view.

IV

The butterfly, safe under leaf and flower,
  Has found a roof, knowing how true thou art;
The bumble-bee, within the last half-hour,
  Has ceased to hug the honey to its heart;
  While in the barnyard, under shed and cart,
Brood-hens have housed.--But I, who scorned thy power,
  Barometer of the birds,--like August there,--
  Beneath a beech, dripping from foot to hair,
        Like some drenched truant, cower.

The
Harvest Moon

I

Globed in Heav'n's tree of azure, golden mellow
  As some round apple hung
High in hesperian boughs, thou hangest yellow
  The branch-like mists among:
Within thy light a sunburnt youth, named Health,
  Rests 'mid the tasseled shocks, the tawny stubble;
And by his side, clad on with rustic wealth
  Of field and farm, beneath thy amber bubble,
A nut-brown maid, Content, sits smiling still:
  While through the quiet trees,
  The mossy rocks, the grassy hill,
Thy silvery spirit glides to yonder mill,
  Around whose wheel the breeze
And shimmering ripples of the water play,
As, by their mother, little children may.

II

Sweet spirit of the moon, who walkest,--lifting
  Exhaustless on thy arm,
A pearly vase of fire,--through the shifting
  Cloud-halls of calm and storm,
Pour down thy blossoms! let me hear them come,

Pelting with noiseless light the twinkling thickets,
Making the darkness audible with the hum
  Of many insect creatures, grigs and crickets:
Until it seems the elves hold revelries
  By haunted stream and grove;
  Or, in the night's deep peace,
The young-old presence of Earth's full increase
  Seems telling thee her love,
Ere, lying down, she turns to rest, and smiles,
Hearing thy heart beat through the myriad miles.

The Old
Water-Mill

Wild ridge on ridge the wooded hills arise,
Between whose breezy vistas gulfs of skies
Pilot great clouds like towering argosies,
And hawk and buzzard breast the azure breeze.
With many a foaming fall and glimmering reach
Of placid murmur, under elm and beech,
The creek goes twinkling through long glows and glooms
Of woodland quiet, poppied with perfumes:
The creek, in whose clear shallows minnow-schools
Glitter or dart; and by whose deeper pools
The blue kingfishers and the herons haunt;
That, often startled from the freckled flaunt
Of blackberry-lilies--where they feed and hide--
Trail a lank flight along the forestside

With eery clangor. Here a sycamore,
Smooth, wave-uprooted, builds from shore to shore
A headlong bridge; and there, a storm-hurled oak
Lays a long dam, where sand and gravel choke
The water's lazy way. Here mistflower blurs
Its bit of heaven; there the oxeye stirs
Its gloaming hues of bronze and gold; and here,
A gray cool stain, like dawn's own atmosphere,
The dim wild-carrot lifts its crumpled crest:
And over all, at slender flight or rest,
The dragon-flies, like coruscating rays
Of lapis-lazuli and chrysoprase,
Drowsily sparkle through the summer days;
And, dewlap-deep, here from the noontide heat
The bell-hung cattle find a cool retreat:
And through the willows girdling the hill,
Now far, now near, borne as the soft winds will,
Comes the low rushing of the water-mill.
Ah, lovely to me from a little child,
How changed the place! wherein once, undefiled,
The glad communion of the sky and stream
Went with me like a presence and a dream.
Where once the brambled meads and orchardlands
Poured ripe abundance down with mellow hands
Of summer; and the birds of field and wood
Called to me in a tongue I understood;
And in the tangles of the old rail-fence
Even the insect tumult had some sense,
And every sound a happy eloquence;
And more to me than wisest books can teach,
The wind and water said; whose words did reach
My soul, addressing their magnificent speech,
Raucous and rushing, from the old mill-wheel,

That made the rolling mill-cogs snore and reel,
Like some old ogre in a fairy-tale
Nodding above his meat and mug of ale.

How memory takes me back the ways that lead--
As when a boy--through woodland and through mead!
To orchards fruited; or to fields in bloom;
Or briary fallows, like a mighty room,
Through which the winds swing censers of perfume,
And where deep blackberries spread miles of fruit;--
A splendid feast, that stayed the ploughboy's foot
When to the tasseling acres of the corn
He drove his team, fresh in the primrose morn;
And from the liberal banquet, nature lent,
Took dewy handfuls as he whistling went.--
A boy once more I stand with sunburnt feet
And watch the harvester sweep down the wheat;
Or laze with warm limbs in the unstacked straw
Nearby the thresher, whose insatiate maw
Devours the sheaves, hot drawling out its hum--
Like some great sleepy bee, above a bloom,
Made drunk with honey--while, grown big with grain,
The bulging sacks receive the golden rain.
Again I tread the valley, sweet with hay,
And hear the bob-white calling far away,
Or wood-dove cooing in the elder-brake;
Or see the sassafras bushes madly shake
As swift, a rufous instant, in the glen
The red-fox leaps and gallops to his den;
Or, standing in the violet-colored gloam,
Hear roadways sound with holiday riding home
From church, or fair, or bounteous barbecue,
Which the whole country to some village drew.

How spilled with berries were its summer hills,
And strewn with walnuts were its autumn rills--
And chestnut burs! fruit of the spring's long flowers,
When from their tops the trees seemed streaming showers
Of slender silver, cool, crepuscular,
And like a nebulous radiance shone afar.
And maples! how their sappy hearts would gush
Broad troughs of syrup, when the winter bush
Steamed with the sugar-kettle, day and night,
And all the snow was streaked with firelight.
Then it was glorious! the mill-dam's edge,
One slant of frosty crystal, laid a ledge
Of pearl across; above which, sleeted trees
Tossed arms of ice, that, clashing in the breeze,
Tinkled the ringing creek with icicles,
Thin as the peal of Elfland's Sabbath bells:
A sound that in my city dreams I hear,
That brings before me, under skies that clear,
The old mill in its winter garb of snow,
Its frozen wheel, a great hoar beard below,
And its West windows, two deep eyes aglow.

Ah, ancient mill, still do I picture o'er
Thy cobwebbed stairs and loft and grain-strewn floor;
Thy door,--like some brown, honest hand of toil,
And honorable with labor of the soil,--
Forever open; through which, on his back
The prosperous farmer bears his bursting sack.
And while the miller measures out his toll,
Again I hear, above the cogs' loud roll,--
That makes stout joist and rafter groan and sway,--
The harmless gossip of the passing day:

Good country talk, that tells how so-and-so
Has died or married; how curculio
And codling-moth have ruined half the fruit,
And blight plays mischief with the grapes to boot;
Or what the news from town; next county fair;
How well the crops are looking everywhere:
Now this, now that, on which their interests fix,
Prospects for rain or frost, and politics.
While, all around, the sweet smell of the meal
Filters, warm-pouring from the grinding wheel
Into the bin; beside which, mealy white,
The miller looms, dim in the dusty light.

Again I see the miller's home, between
The crinkling creek and hills of beechen green:
Again the miller greets me, gaunt and brown,
Who oft o'erawed me with his gray-browed frown
And rugged mien: again he tries to reach
My youthful mind with fervid scriptural speech.--
For he, of all the country-side confessed,
The most religious was and happiest;
A Methodist, and one whom faith still led,
No books except the Bible had he read--
At least so seemed it to my younger head.--
All things in earth and heav'n he'd prove by this,
Be it a fact or mere hypothesis;
For to his simple wisdom, reverent,
"*The Bible says*" was all of argument.--
God keep his soul! his bones were long since laid
Among the sunken gravestones in the shade
Of those black-lichened rocks, that wall around
The family burying-ground with cedars crowned;
Where bristling teasel and the brier combine

With clambering wood-rose and the wild-grape vine
To hide the stone whereon his name and dates
Neglect, with mossy hand, obliterates.

Anthem
of Dawn

I

Then up the orient heights to the zenith, that balanced the crescent,--
Up and far up and over,--the heaven grew erubescent,
Vibrant with rose and with ruby from the hands of the harpist Dawn,
Smiting symphonic fire on the firmament's barbiton:
And the East was a priest who adored with offerings of gold and of gems,
And a wonderful carpet unrolled for the inaccessible hems
Of the glistening robes of her limbs; that, lily and amethyst,
Swept glorying on and on through temples of cloud and mist.

II

Then out of the splendor and richness, that burned like a magic stone,
The torrent suffusion that deepened and dazzled and broadened and shone,
The pomp and the pageant of color, triumphal procession of glare,
The sun, like a king in armor, breathing splendor from feet to hair,
Stood forth with majesty girdled, as a hero who towers afar
Where the bannered gates are bristling hells and the walls are roaring war:

And broad on the back of the world, like a Cherubin's fiery blade,
The effulgent gaze of his aspect fell in glittering accolade.

III

Then billowing blue, like an ocean, rolled from the shores of morn to even:
And the stars, like rafts, went down: and the moon, like a ghost-ship, driven,
A feather of foam, from port to port of the cloud-built isles that dotted,
With pearl and cameo, bays of the day, her canvas webbed and rotted,
Lay lost in the gulf of heaven: while over her mixed and melted
The beautiful children of Morn, whose bodies are opal-belted;
The beautiful daughters of Dawn, who, over and under, and after
The rivered radiance, wrestled; and rainbowed heaven with laughter
Of halcyon sapphire.--O Dawn! thou visible mirth,
And hallelujah of Heaven! hosanna of Earth!

Dithyrambics

I

TEMPEST

Wrapped round of the night, as a monster is wrapped of the ocean,
Down, down through vast storeys of darkness, behold, in the tower
Of the heaven, the thunder! on stairways of cloudy commotion,
Colossal of tread, like a giant, from echoing hour to hour
Goes striding in rattling armor ...

The Nymph, at her billow-roofed dormer
Of foam; and the Sylvan--green-housed--at her window of leaves appears;
--As a listening woman, who hears
The approach of her lover, who comes to her arms in the night;
And, loosening the loops of her locks,
With eyes full of love and delight,
From the couch of her rest in ardor and haste arises.--
The Nymph, as if breathed of the tempest, like fire surprises
The riotous bands of the rocks,
That face with a roar the shouting charge of the seas.
The Sylvan,--through troops of the trees,
Whose clamorous clans with gnarly bosoms keep hurling
Themselves on the guns of the wind,--goes wheeling and whirling.
The Nymph, of the waves' exultation upheld, her green tresses
Knotted with flowers of the hollow white foam, dives screaming;
Then bounds to the arms of the storm, who boisterously presses
Her hair and wild form to his breast that is panting and streaming.
The Sylvan,--hard-pressed by the wind, the Pan-footed air,--
On the violent backs of the hills,--
Like a flame that tosses and thrills
From peak to peak when the world of spirits is out,--
Is borne, as her rapture wills,
With glittering gesture and shout:
Now here in the darkness, now there,
From the rain-like sweep of her hair,--
Bewilderingly volleyed o'er eyes and o'er lips,--
To the lambent swell of her limbs, her breasts and her hips,
She flashes her beautiful nakedness out in the glare
Of the tempest that bears her away,--
That bears me away!
Away, over forest and foam, over tree and spray,
Far swifter than thought, far swifter than sound or than flame.
Over ocean and pine,

In arms of tumultuous shadow and shine ...
Though Sylvan and Nymph do not
Exist, and only what
Of terror and beauty I feel and I name
As parts of the storm, the awe and the rapture divine
That here in the tempest are mine,--
The two are the same, the two are forever the same.

II

CALM

Beautiful-bosomed, O night, in thy noon
Move with majesty onward! bearing, as lightly
As a singer may bear the notes of an exquisite tune,
The stars and the moon
Through the clerestories high of the heaven, the firmament's halls;
Under whose sapphirine walls,
June, hesperian June,
Robed in divinity wanders. Daily and nightly
The turquoise touch of her robe, that the violets star,
The silvery fall of her feet, that lilies are,
Fill the land with languorous light and perfume.--
Is it the melody mute of burgeoning leaf and of bloom?
The music of Nature, that silently shapes in the gloom
Immaterial hosts
Of spirits that have the flowers and leaves in their keep,
That I hear, that I hear?
Invisible ghosts,--
Who whisper in leaves and glimmer in blossoms and hover
In color and fragrance and loveliness, breathed from the deep

World-soul of the mother,
Nature;--who, over and over,
Both sweetheart and lover,
Goes singing her songs from one sweet month to the other,--
That appear, that appear?
In forest and field, on hill-land and lea,
As crystallized harmony,
Materialized melody,
An uttered essence peopling far and near
The hyaline atmosphere?...
Behold how it sprouts from the grass and blooms from flower and tree!
In waves of diaphanous moonlight and mist,
In fugue upon fugue of gold and of amethyst,
Around me, above me it spirals; now slower, now faster,
Like symphonies born of the thought of a musical master.--
--O music of Earth! O God who the music inspired!
Let me breathe of the life of thy breath!
And so be fulfilled and attired
In resurrection, triumphant o'er time and o'er death!

Hymn to
Desire

I

Mother of visions, with lineaments dulcet as numbers
Breathed on the eyelids of love by music that slumbers,
Secretly, sweetly, O presence of fire and snow,
Thou comest mysterious,
In beauty imperious,
Clad on with dreams and the light of no world that we know.
Deep to my innermost soul am I shaken,
Helplessly shaken and tossed,
And of thy tyrannous yearnings so utterly taken,
My lips, unsatisfied, thirst;
Mine eyes are accurst
With longings for visions that far in the night are forsaken;
And mine ears, in listening lost,
Yearn, yearn for the note of a chord that will never awaken.

II

Like palpable music thou comest, like moonlight; and far,--
Resonant bar upon bar,--
The vibrating lyre
Of the spirit responds with melodious fire,
As thy fluttering fingers now grasp it and ardently shake,
With flame and with flake,

The chords of existence, the instrument star-sprung.
Whose frame is of clay, so wonderfully molded from mire.

III

Vested with vanquishment, come, O Desire, Desire!
Breathe in this harp of my soul the audible angel of love!
Make of my heart an Israfel burning above,
A lute for the music of God, that lips, which are mortal, but stammer!
Smite every rapturous wire
With golden delirium, rebellion and silvery clamor,
Crying--"Awake! awake!
Too long hast thou slumbered! too far from the regions of glamour,
With its mountains of magic, its fountains of Faery, the spar-sprung,
Hast thou wandered away, O Heart!
Come, oh, come and partake
Of necromance banquets of beauty; and slake
Thy thirst in the waters of art,
That are drawn from the streams
Of love and of dreams."

IV

"Come, oh, come!
No longer shall language be dumb!
Thy vision shall grasp--
As one doth the glittering hasp
Of a dagger made splendid with gems and with gold--
The wonder and richness of life, not anguish and hate of it merely.

And out of the stark
Eternity, awful and dark,
Immensity silent and cold,--
Universe-shaking as trumpets, or thunderous metals
That cymbal; yet pensive and pearly
And soft as the rosy unfolding of petals,
Or crumbling aroma of blossoms that wither too early,--
The majestic music of Death, where he plays
On the organ of eons and days."

Music

Thou, oh, thou!
Thou of the chorded shell and golden plectrum! thou
Of the dark eyes and pale pacific brow!
Music, who by the plangent waves,
Or in the echoing night of labyrinthine caves,
Or on God's mountains, lonely as the stars,
Touchest reverberant bars
Of immemorial sorrow and amaze;--
Keeping regret and memory awake,
And all the immortal ache
Of love that leans upon the past's sweet days
In retrospection!--now, oh, now,
Interpreter and heart-physician, thou,
Who gazest on the heaven and the hell
Of life, and singest each as well,
Touch with thy all-mellifluous finger-tips,
Or thy melodious lips,

This sickness named my soul,
Making it whole,
As is an echo of a chord,
Or some symphonic word,
Or sweet vibrating sigh,
That deep, resurgent still doth rise and die
On thy voluminous roll;
Part of the beauty and the mystery
That axles Earth with song; and as a slave,
Swings it around and 'round on each sonorous pole,
'Mid spheric harmony,
And choral majesty,
And diapasoning of wind and wave;
And speeds it on its far elliptic way
'Mid vasty anthemings of night and day.--
O cosmic cry
Of two eternities, wherein we see
The phantasms, Death and Life,
At endless strife
Above the silence of a monster grave.

Jotunheim

I

Beyond the Northern Lights, in regions haunted
Of twilight, where the world is glacier planted,
And pale as Loki in his cavern when
The serpent's slaver burns him to the bones,

I saw the phantasms of gigantic men,
The prototypes of vastness, quarrying stones;
Great blocks of winter, glittering with the morn's
And evening's colors,--wild prismatic tones
Of boreal beauty.--Like the three gray Norns,
Silence and solitude and terror loomed
Around them where they labored. Walls arose,
Vast as the Andes when creation boomed
Insurgent fire; and through the rushing snows
Enormous battlements of tremendous ice,
Bastioned and turreted, I saw arise.

II

But who can sing the workmanship gigantic
  That reared within its coruscating dome
The roaring fountain, hurling an Atlantic
  Of streaming ice that flashed with flame and foam?
An opal spirit, various and many formed,--
In whose clear heart reverberant fire stormed,--
  Seemed its inhabitant; and through pale halls,
    And deep diaphanous walls,
    And corridors of whiteness.
    Auroral colors swarmed,
    As rosy-flickering stains,
Or lambent green, or gold, or crimson, warmed
The pulsing crystal of the spirit's veins
    With ever-changing brightness.
And through the Arctic night there went a voice,
As if the ancient Earth cried out, "Rejoice!
    My heart is full of lightness!"

III

Here well might Thor, the god of war,
Harness the whirlwinds to his car,
While, mailed in storm, his iron arm
Heaves high his hammer's lava-form,
And red and black his beard streams back,
Like some fierce torrent scoriac,
Whose earthquake light glares through the night
Around some dark volcanic height;
And through the skies Valkyrian cries
Trumpet, as battleward he flies,
Death in his hair and havoc in his eyes.

IV

Still in my dreams I hear that fountain flowing;
Beyond all seeing and beyond all knowing;
Still in my dreams I see those wild walls glowing
  With hues, Aurora-kissed;
And through huge halls fantastic phantoms going.
  Vast shapes of snow and mist,--
Sonorous clarions of the tempest blowing,--
  That trail dark banners by,
  Cloudlike, underneath the sky
  Of the caverned dome on high,
  Carbuncle and amethyst.--
  Still I hear the ululation
  Of their stormy exultation,
  Multitudinous, and blending

In hoarse echoes, far, unending;
And, through halls of fog and frost,
Howling back, like madness lost
In the moonless mansion of
Its own demon-haunted love.

V

Still in my dreams I hear the mermaid singing;
The mermaid music at its portal ringing;
The mermaid song, that hinged with gold its door,
   And, whispering evermore,
   Hushed the ponderous hurl and roar
   And vast aeolian thunder
   Of the chained tempests under
   The frozen cataracts that were its floor.--
And, blinding beautiful, I still behold
The mermaid there, combing her locks of gold,
While, at her feet, green as the Northern Seas,
Gambol her flocks of seals and walruses;
While, like a drift, her dog--a Polar bear--
Lies by her, glowering through his shaggy hair.

VI

O wondrous house, built by supernal hands
   In vague and ultimate lands!
Thy architects were behemoth wind and cloud,
   That, laboring loud,

Mountained thy world foundations and uplifted
  Thy skyey bastions drifted
Of piled eternities of ice and snow;
  Where storms, like ploughmen, go,
Ploughing the deeps with awful hurricane;
  Where, spouting icy rain,
The huge whale wallows; and through furious hail
  Th' explorer's tattered sail
Drives like the wing of some terrific bird,
  Where wreck and famine herd.--
Home of the red Auroras and the gods!
He who profanes thy perilous threshold,--where
  The ancient centuries lair,
And, glacier-throned, thy monarch, Winter, nods,--
  Let him beware!
Lest, coming on that hoary presence there,
  Whose pitiless hand,
  Above that hungry land,
An iceberg wields as sceptre, and whose crown
  The North Star is, set in a band of frost,
He, too, shall feel the bitterness of that frown,
  And, turned to stone, forevermore be lost.

Dionysia

The day is dead; and in the west
The slender crescent of the moon--
Diana's crystal-kindled crest--
Sinks hillward in a silvery swoon.
What is the murmur in the dell?
The stealthy whisper and the drip?--
A Dryad with her leaf-light trip?
Or Naiad o'er her fountain well?--
Who, with white fingers for her comb,
Sleeks her blue hair, and from its curls
Showers slim minnows and pale pearls,
And hollow music of the foam.
What is it in the vistaed ways
That leans and springs, and stoops and sways?--
The naked limbs of one who flees?
An Oread who hesitates
Before the Satyr form that waits,
Crouching to leap, that there she sees?
Or under boughs, reclining cool,
A Hamadryad, like a pool
Of moonlight, palely beautiful?
Or Limnad, with her lilied face,
More lovely than the misty lace
That haunts a star and gives it grace?
Or is it some Leimoniad,
In wildwood flowers dimly clad?
Oblong blossoms white as froth;
Or mottled like the tiger-moth;
Or brindled as the brows of death;

Wild of hue and wild of breath.
Here ethereal flame and milk
Blent with velvet and with silk;
Here an iridescent glow
Mixed with satin and with snow:
Pansy, poppy and the pale
Serpolet and galingale;
Mandrake and anemone,
Honey-reservoirs o' the bee;
Cistus and the cyclamen,--
Cheeked like blushing Hebe this,
And the other white as is
Bubbled milk of Venus when
Cupid's baby mouth is pressed,
Rosy, to her rosy breast.
And, besides, all flowers that mate
With aroma, and in hue
Stars and rainbows duplicate
Here on earth for me and you.

Yea! at last mine eyes can see!
'Tis no shadow of the tree
Swaying softly there, but she!--
Maenad, Bassarid, Bacchant,
What you will, who doth enchant
Night with sensuous nudity.
Lo! again I hear her pant
Breasting through the dewy glooms--
Through the glow-worm gleams and glowers
Of the starlight;--wood-perfumes
Swoon around her and frail showers
Of the leaflet-tilted rain.
Lo, like love, she comes again,

Through the pale, voluptuous dusk,
Sweet of limb with breasts of musk.
With her lips, like blossoms, breathing
Honeyed pungence of her kiss,
And her auburn tresses wreathing
Like umbrageous helichrys,
There she stands, like fire and snow,
In the moon's ambrosial glow,
Both her shapely loins low-looped
With the balmy blossoms, drooped,
Of the deep amaracus.
Spiritual yet sensual,
Lo, she ever greets me thus
In my vision; white and tall,
Her delicious body there,--
Raimented with amorous air,--
To my mind expresses all
The allurements of the world.
And once more I seem to feel
On my soul, like frenzy, hurled
All the passionate past.--I reel,
Greek again in ancient Greece,
In the Pyrrhic revelries;
In the mad and Maenad dance
Onward dragged with violence;
Pan and old Silenus and
Faunus and a Bacchant band
Round me. Wild my wine-stained hand
O'er tumultuous hair is lifted;
While the flushed and Phallic orgies
Whirl around me; and the marges
Of the wood are torn and rifted
With lascivious laugh and shout.

And barbarian there again,--
Shameless with the shameless rout,
Bacchus lusting in each vein,--
With her pagan lips on mine,
Like a god made drunk with wine,
On I reel; and, in the revels,
Her loose hair, the dance dishevels,
Blows, and 'thwart my vision swims
All the splendor of her limbs....

So it seems. Yet woods are lonely.
And when I again awake,
I shall find their faces only
Moonbeams in the boughs that shake;
And their revels, but the rush
Of night-winds through bough and brush.
Yet my dreaming--is it more
Than mere dreaming? Is some door
Opened in my soul? a curtain
Raised? to let me see for certain
I have lived that life before?

The Last
Song

She sleeps; he sings to her. The day was long,
And, tired out with too much happiness,
She fain would have him sing of old Provence;
Quaint songs, that spoke of love in such soft tones,
Her restless soul was straight besieged of dreams,
And her wild heart beleagured of deep peace,
And heart and soul surrendered unto sleep.--
Like perfect sculpture in the moon she lies,
Its pallor on her through heraldic panes
Of one tall casement's guled quarterings.--
Beside her couch, an antique table, weighed
With gold and crystal; here, a carven chair,
Whereon her raiment,--that suggests sweet curves
Of shapely beauty,--bearing her limbs' impress,
Is richly laid: and, near the chair, a glass,
An oval mirror framed in ebony:
And, dim and deep,--investing all the room
With ghostly life of woven women and men,
And strange fantastic gloom, where shadows live,--
Dark tapestry,--which in the gusts--that twinge
A grotesque cresset's slender star of light--
Seems moved of cautious hands, assassin-like,
That wait the hour.
                She alone, deep-haired
As rosy dawn, and whiter than a rose,
Divinely breasted as the Queen of Love,
Lies robeless in the glimmer of the moon,

Like Danae within the golden shower.
Seated beside her aromatic rest,
In rapture musing on her loveliness,
Her knight and troubadour. A lute, aslope
The curious baldric of his tunic, glints
With pearl-reflections of the moon, that seem
The silent ghosts of long-dead melodies.
In purple and sable, slashed with solemn gold,
Like stately twilight o'er the snow-heaped hills,
He bends above her.--
              Have his hands forgot
Their craft, that they pause, idle on the strings?
His lips, their art, that they cease, speechless there?--
His eyes are set.... What is it stills to stone
His hands, his lips? and mails him, head and heel,
In terrible marble, motionless and cold?--
Behind the arras, can it be he feels,
Black-browed and grim, with eyes of sombre fire,
Death towers above him with uplifted sword?

Romaunt of
the Oak

"I rode to death, for I fought for shame--
The Lady Maurine of noble name,

"The fair and faithless!--Though life be long
Is love the wiser?--Love made song

"Of all my life; and the soul that crept
Before, arose like a star and leapt:

"Still leaps with the love that it found untrue,
That it found unworthy.--Now run me through!

"Yea, run me through! for meet and well,
And a jest for laughter of fiends in hell,

"It is that I, who have done no wrong,
Should die by the hand of Hugh the Strong,

"Of Hugh her leman!--What else could be
When the devil was judge twixt thee and me?

"He splintered my lance, and my blade he broke--
Now finish me thou 'neath the trysting oak!" ...

The crest of his foeman,--a heart of white
In a bath of fire,--stooped i' the night;

Stooped and laughed as his sword he swung,
Then galloped away with a laugh on his tongue....

But who is she in the gray, wet dawn,
'Mid the autumn shades like a shadow wan?

Who kneels, one hand on her straining breast,
One hand on the dead man's bosom pressed?

Her face is dim as the dead's; as cold
As his tarnished harness of steel and gold.

O Lady Maurine! O Lady Maurine!
What boots it now that regret is keen?

That his hair you smooth, that you kiss his brow
What boots it now? what boots it now?...

She has haled him under the trysting oak,
The huge old oak that the creepers cloak.

She has stood him, gaunt in his battered arms,
In its haunted hollow.--"Be safe from storms,"

She laughed as his cloven casque she placed
On his brow, and his riven shield she braced.

Then sat and talked to the forest flowers
Through the lonely term of the day's pale hours.

And stared and whispered and smiled and wept,
While nearer and nearer the evening crept.

And, lo, when the moon, like a great gold bloom
Above the sorrowful trees did loom,

She rose up sobbing, "O moon, come see
My bridegroom here in the old oak-tree!

"I have talked to the flowers all day, all day,
For never a word had he to say.

"He would not listen, he would not hear,
Though I wailed my longing into his ear.

"O moon, steal in where he stands so grim,
And tell him I love him, and plead with him.

"Soften his face that is cold and stern
And brighten his eyes and make them burn,

"O moon, O moon, so my soul can see
That his heart still glows with love for me!" ...

When the moon was set, and the woods were dark,
The wild deer came and stood as stark

As phantoms with eyes of fire; or fled
Like a ghostly hunt of the herded dead.

And the hoot-owl called; and the were-wolf snarled;
And a voice, in the boughs of the oak-tree gnarled,--

Like the whining rush of the hags that ride
To the witches' sabboth,--crooned and cried.

And wrapped in his mantle of wind and cloud
The storm-fiend stalked through the forest loud.

When she heard the dead man rattle and groan
As the oak was bent and its leaves were blown,

And the lightning vanished and shimmered his mail,
Through the swirling sweep of the rain and hail,

She seemed to hear him, who seemed to call,--
"Come hither, Maurine, the wild leaves fall!

"The wild leaves rustle, the wild leaves flee;
Come hither, Maurine, to the hollow tree!

"To the trysting tree, to the tree once green;
Come hither, Maurine! come hither, Maurine!" ...

They found her closed in his armored arms--
Had he claimed his bride on that night of storms?

Morgan le
Fay

In dim samite was she bedight,
  And on her hair a hoop of gold,
Like fox-fire in the tawn moonlight,
  Was glimmering cold.

With soft gray eyes she gloomed and glowered;
  With soft red lips she sang a song:
What knight might gaze upon her face,
  Nor fare along?

For all her looks were full of spells,
  And all her words of sorcery;
And in some way they seemed to say
  "Oh, come with me!

"Oh, come with me! oh, come with me!
  Oh, come with me, my love, Sir Kay!"--
How should he know the witch, I trow,
  Morgan le Fay?

How should he know the wily witch,
  With sweet white face and raven hair?
Who by her art bewitched his heart
  And held him there.

For soul and sense had waxed amort
  To wold and weald, to slade and stream;

And all he heard was her soft word
　　As one adream.

And all he saw was her bright eyes,
　　And her fair face that held him still;
And wild and wan she led him on
　　O'er vale and hill.

Until at last a castle lay
　　Beneath the moon, among the trees;
Its Gothic towers old and gray
　　With mysteries.

Tall in its hall an hundred knights
　　In armor stood with glaive in hand;
The following of some great King,
　　Lord of that land.

Sir Bors, Sir Balin, and Gawain,
　　All Arthur's knights, and many mo;
But these in battle had been slain
　　Long years ago.

But when Morgan with lifted hand
　　Moved down the hall, they louted low;
For she was Queen of Shadowland,
　　That woman of snow.

Then from Sir Kay she drew away,
　　And mocking at him by her side,--
"Behold, Sir Knights, the knave who slew
　　Your King," she cried.

Then like one man those shadows raised
  Their swords, whereon the moon glanced gray;
And clashing all strode from the wall
  Against Sir Kay.

And on his body, bent and bowed,
  The hundred blades like one blade fell;
While over all rang long and loud
  The mirth of Hell.

The Dream
of Roderick

Below, the tawny Tagus swept
Past royal gardens, breathing balm;
Upon his couch the monarch slept;
The world was still; the night was calm.

Gray, Gothic-gated, in the ray
Of moonrise, tower-and castle-crowned,
The city of Toledo lay
Beneath the terraced palace-ground.

Again, he dreamed, in kingly sport
He sought the tree-sequestered path,
And watched the ladies of his Court
Within the marble-basined bath.

Its porphyry stairs and fountained base
Shone, houried with voluptuous forms,
Where Andalusia vied in grace
With old Castile, in female charms.

And laughter, song, and water-splash
Rang round the place, with stone arcaded,
As here a breast or limb would flash
Where beauty swam or beauty waded.

And then, like Venus, from the wave
A maiden came, and stood below;
And by her side a woman slave
Bent down to dry her limbs of snow.

Then on the tesselated bank,
Robed on with fragrance and with fire,--
Like some exotic flower--she sank,
The type of all divine desire.

Then her dark curls, that sparkled wet,
She parted from her perfect brows,
And, lo, her eyes, like lamps of jet
Within an alabaster house.

And in his sleep the monarch sighed,
"Florinda!"--Dreaming still he moaned,
"Ah, would that I had died, had died!
I have atoned! I have atoned!" ...

And then the vision changed: O'erhead
Tempest and darkness were unrolled,
Full of wild voices of the dead,

And lamentations manifold.

And wandering shapes of gaunt despair
Swept by, with faces pale as pain,
Whose eyes wept blood and seemed to glare
Fierce curses on him through the rain.

And then, it seemed, 'gainst blazing skies
A necromantic tower sate,
Crag-like on crags, of giant size;
Of adamant its walls and gate.

And from the storm a hand of might
Red-rolled in thunder, reached among
The gate's huge bolts--that burst; and night
Clanged ruin as its hinges swung.

Then far away a murmur trailed,--
As of sad seas on cavern'd shores,--
That grew into a voice that wailed,
"They come! they come! the Moors! the Moors!"

And with deep boom of atabals
And crash of cymbals and wild peal
Of battle-bugles, from its walls
An army rushed in glimmering steel.

And where it trod he saw the torch
Of conflagration stalk the skies,
And in the vanward of its march
The monster form of Havoc rise.

And Paynim war-cries rent the storm,
Athwart whose firmament of flame,
Destruction reared an earthquake form
On wreck and death without a name ...

And then again the vision changed:
Where flows the Guadalete, see,
The warriors of the Cross are ranged
Against the Crescent's chivalry.

With roar of trumpets and of drums
They meet; and in the battle's van
He fights; and, towering towards him, comes
Florinda's father, Julian;

And one-eyed Taric, great in war:
And where these couch their burning spears,
The Christian phalanx, near and far,
Goes down like corn before the shears.

The Moslem wins: the Christian flies:
"Allah il Allah," hill and plain
Reverberate: the rocking skies,
"Allah il Allah," shout again.

And then he dreamed the swing of swords
And hurl of arrows were no more;
But, louder than the howling hordes,
Strange silence fell on field and shore.

And through the night, it seemed, he fled,
Upon a white steed like a star,
Across a field of endless dead,

Beneath a blood-red scimitar.

Of sunset: And he heard a moan,
Beneath, around, on every hand--
"Accursed! Yea, what hast thou done
To bring this curse upon thy land?"

And then an awful sense of wings:
And, lo! the answer--"'Twas his lust
That was his crime. Behold! E'en kings
Must reckon with Me. All are dust."

Zyps of
Zirl

The Alps of the Tyrol are dark with pines,
Where, foaming under the mountain spines,
The Inn's long water sounds and shines.

Beyond, are peaks where the morning weaves
An icy rose; and the evening leaves
The glittering gold of a thousand sheaves.

Deep vines and torrents and glimmering haze,
And sheep-bells tinkling on mountain ways,
And fluting shepherds make sweet the days.

The rolling mist, like a wandering fleece,

The great round moon in a mountain crease,
And a song of love make the nights all peace.

Beneath the blue Tyrolean skies
On the banks of the Inn, that foams and flies,
The storied city of Innsbruck lies.

With its mediaeval streets, that crook,
And its gabled houses, it has the look
Of a belfried town in a fairy-book.

So wild the Tyrol that oft, 'tis said,
When the storm is out and the town in bed,
The howling of wolves sweeps overhead.

And oft the burgher, sitting here
In his walled rose-garden, hears the clear
Shrill scream of the eagle circling near.

And this is the tale that the burghers tell:--
The Abbot of Wiltau stood at his cell
Where the Solstein lifts its pinnacle.

A mighty summit of bluffs and crags
That frowns on the Inn; where the forest stags
Have worn a path to the water-flags.

The Abbot of Wiltau stood below;
And he was aware of a plume and bow
On the precipice there in the morning's glow.

A chamois, he saw, from span to span
Had leapt; and after it leapt a man;

And he knew 't was the Kaiser Maxmilian.

But, see! though rash as the chamois he,
His foot less sure. And verily
If the King should miss ... "Jesu, Marie!

"The King hath missed!"--And, look, he falls!
Rolls headlong out to the headlong walls.
What saint shall save him on whom he calls?

What saint shall save him, who struggles there
On the narrow ledge by the eagle's lair,
With hooked hands clinging 'twixt earth and air?

The Abbot, he crosses himself in dread--
"Let prayers go up for the nearly dead,
And the passing-bell be tolled," he said.

"For the House of Hapsburg totters; see,
How raveled the thread of its destiny,
Sheer hung between cloud and rock!" quoth he.

But hark! where the steeps of the peak reply,
Is it an eagle's echoing cry?
And the flitting shadow, its plumes on high?

No voice of the eagle is that which rings!
And the shadow, a wiry man who swings
Down, down where the desperate Kaiser clings.

The ***crampons*** bound to his feet, he leaps
Like a chamois now; and again he creeps
Or twists, like a snake, o'er the fearful deeps.

"By his cross-bow, baldrick, and cap's black curl,"
Quoth the Abbot below, "I know the churl!
'T is the hunted outlaw Zyps of Zirl.

"Upon whose head, or dead or alive,
The Kaiser hath posted a price.--Saints shrive
The King!" quoth Wiltau. "Who may contrive

"To save him now that his foe is there?"--
But, listen! again through the breathless air
What words are those that the echoes bear?

"Courage, my King!--To the rescue, ho!"
The wild voice rings like a twanging bow,
And the staring Abbot stands mute below.

And, lo! the hand of the outlaw grasps
The arm of the King--and death unclasps
Its fleshless fingers from him who gasps.

And how he guides! where the clean cliffs wedge
Them flat to their faces; by chasm and ledge
He helps the King from the merciless edge.

Then up and up, past bluffs that shun
The rashest chamois; where eagles sun
Fierce wings and brood; where the mists are spun.

And safe at last stand Kaiser and churl
On the mountain path where the mosses curl--
And this the revenge of Zyps of Zirl.

The
Glowworm

How long had I sat there and had not beheld
The gleam of the glow-worm till something compelled!...

The heaven was starless, the forest was deep,
And the vistas of darkness stretched silent in sleep.

And late 'mid the trees had I lingered until
No thing was awake but the lone whippoorwill.

And haunted of thoughts for an hour I sat
On a lichen-gray rock where the moss was a mat.

And thinking of one whom my heart had held dear,
Like terrible waters, a gathering fear.

Came stealing upon me with all the distress
Of loss and of yearning and powerlessness:

Till the hopes and the doubts and the sleepless unrest
That, swallow-like, built in the home of my breast,

Now hither, now thither, now heavenward flew,
Wild-winged as the winds are: now suddenly drew

My soul to abysses of nothingness where
All light was a shadow, all hope, a despair:

Where truth, that religion had set upon high,
The darkness distorted and changed to a lie:

And dreams of the beauty ambition had fed
Like leaves of the autumn fell blighted and dead.

And I rose with my burden of anguish and doom,
And cried, "O my God, had I died in the womb!

"Than born into night, with no hope of the morn,
An heir unto shadows, to live so forlorn!

"All effort is vain; and the planet called Faith
Sinks down; and no power is real but death.

"Oh, light me a torch in the deepening dark
So my sick soul may follow, my sad heart may mark!"--

And then in the darkness the answer!--It came
From Earth not from Heaven--a glimmering flame,

Behold, at my feet! In the shadow it shone
Mysteriously lovely and dimly alone:

An ember; a sparkle of dew and of glower;
Like the lamp that a spirit hangs under a flower:

As goldenly green as the phosphorus star
A fairy may wear in her diadem's bar:

An element essence of moonlight and dawn
That, trodden and trampled, burns on and burns on.

And hushed was my soul with the lesson of light
That God had revealed to me there in the night:

Though mortal its structure, material its form,
The spiritual message of worm unto worm.

Ghosts

Was it the strain of the waltz that, repeating
"Love," so bewitched me? or only the gleam
There of the lustres, that set my heart beating,
Feeling your presence as one feels a dream?

For, on a sudden, the woman of fashion,
Soft at my side in her diamonds and lace,
Vanished, and pale with reproach or with passion,
You, my dead sweetheart, smiled up in my face.

Music, the nebulous lights, and the sifting
Fragrance of women made amorous the air;
Born of these three and my thoughts you came drifting,
Clad in dim muslin, a rose in your hair.

There in the waltz, that followed the lancers,
Hard to my breast did I crush you and hold;
Far through the stir and the throng of the dancers
Onward I bore you as often of old.

Pale were your looks; and the rose in your tresses

Paler of hue than the dreams we have lost;--
"Who," then I said, "is it sees or who guesses,
Here in the hall, that I dance with a ghost?"

Gone! And the dance and the music are ended.
Gone! And the rapture dies out of the skies.
And, on my arm, in her elegance splendid,
The woman of fashion smiles up in my eyes.

Had I forgotten? and did you remember?--
You, who are dead, whom I cannot forget;
You, for whose sake all my heart is an ember
Covered with ashes of dreams and regret.

The Purple Valleys

Far in the purple valleys of illusion
I see her waiting, like the soul of music,
With deep eyes, lovelier than cerulean pansies,
Shadow and fire, yet merciless as poison;
With red lips, sweeter than Arabian storax,
Yet bitterer than myrrh.--O tears and kisses!
O eyes and lips, that haunt my soul forever!

Again Spring walks transcendent on the mountains:
The woods are hushed: the vales are blue with shadows:
Above the heights, steeped in a thousand splendors,

Like some vast canvas of the gods, hangs burning
The sunset's wild sciography: and slowly
The moon treads heaven's proscenium,--night's stately
White queen of love and tragedy and madness.

Again I know forgotten dreams and longings;
Ideals lost; desires dead and buried
Beside the altar sacrifice erected
Within the heart's high sanctuary. Strangely
Again I know the horror and the rapture,
The utterless awe, the joy akin to anguish,
The terror and the worship of the spirit.

Again I feel her eyes pierce through and through me;
Her deep eyes, lovelier than imperial pansies,
Velvet and flame, through which her fierce will holds me,
Powerless and tame, and draws me on and onward
To sad, unsatisfied and animal yearnings,
Wild, unrestrained--the brute within the human--
To fling me panting on her mouth and bosom.

Again I feel her lips like ice and fire,
Her red lips, odorous as Arabian storax,
Fragrance and fire, within whose kiss destruction
Lies serpent-like. Intoxicating languors
Resistlessly embrace me, soul and body;
And we go drifting, drifting--she is laughing--
Outcasts of God, into the deep's abysm.

The Land
of Illusion

I

So we had come at last, my soul and I,
  Into that land of shadowy plain and peak,
  On which the dawn seemed ever about to break
On which the day seemed ever about to die.

II

Long had we sought fulfillment of our dreams,
  The everlasting wells of Joy and Youth;
  Long had we sought the snow-white flow'r of Truth,
That blooms eternal by eternal streams.

III

And, fonder still, we hoped to find the sweet
  Immortal presence, Love; the bird Delight
  Beside her; and, eyed with sidereal night,
Faith, like a lion, fawning at her feet.

IV

But, scorched and barren, in its arid well,
  We found our dreams' forgotten fountain-head;
  And by black, bitter waters, crushed and dead,
Among wild weeds, Truth's trampled asphodel.

V

And side by side with pallid Doubt and Pain,
  Not Love, but Grief did meet us there: afar
  We saw her, like a melancholy star,
Or pensive moon, move towards us o'er the plain.

VI

Sweet was her face as song that sings of home;
  And filled our hearts with vague, suggestive spells
  Of pathos, as sad ocean fills its shells
With sympathetic moanings of its foam.

VII

She raised one hand and pointed silently,
  Then passed; her eyes, gaunt with a thirst unslaked,
  Were worlds of woe, where tears in torrents ached,

Yet never fell. And like a winter sea,--

VIII

Whose caverned crags are haunts of wreck and wrath,
  That house the condor pinions of the storm,--
  My soul replied; and, weeping, arm in arm,
To'ards those dim hills, by that appointed path,

IX

We turned and went. Arrived, we did discern
  How Beauty beckoned, white 'mid miles of flowers,
  Through which, behold, the amaranthine Hours
Like maidens went each holding up an urn;

X

Wherein, it seemed--drained from long chalices
  Of those slim flow'rs--they bore mysterious wine;
  A poppied vintage, full of sleep divine
And pale forgetting of all miseries.

XI

Then to my soul I said, "No longer weep.
  Come, let us drink; for hateful is the sky,
  And earth is full of care, and life's a lie.
So let us drink; yea, let us drink and sleep."

XII

Then from their brimming urns we drank sweet must,
  While, all around us, rose-crowned faces laughed
  Into our eyes; but hardly had we quaffed
When, one by one, these crumbled into dust.

XIII

And league on league the eminence of blooms,
  That flashed and billowed like a summer sea,
  Rolled out a waste of thorns and tombs; where bee
And butterfly and bird hung dead in looms

XIV

Of worm and spider. And through tomb and brier,
  A thin wind, parched with thirsty dust and sand,
  Went wailing as if mourning some lost land

Of perished empire, Babylon or Tyre.

XV

Long, long with blistered feet we wandered in
  That land of ruins, through whose sky of brass
  Hate's Harpy shrieked; and in whose iron grass
The Hydra hissed of undestroyable Sin.

XVI

And there at last, behold, the House of Doom,--
  Red, as if Hell had glared it into life,
  Blood-red, and howling with incessant strife,--
With burning battlements, towered in the gloom.

XVII

And throned within sat Darkness.--Who might gaze
  Upon that form, that threatening presence there,
  Crowned with the flickering corpse-lights of Despair,
And yet escape sans madness and amaze?

XVIII

And we had hoped to find among these hills
  The House of Beauty!--Curst, yea, thrice accurst,
  The hope that lures one on from last to first
With vain illusions that no time fulfills!

XIX

Why will we struggle to attain, and strive,
  When all we gain is but an empty dream?--
  Better, unto my thinking, doth it seem
To end it all and let who will survive;

XX

To find at last all beauty is but dust;
  That love and sorrow are the very same;
  That joy is only suffering's sweeter name;
And sense is but the synonym of lust.

XXI

Far better, yea, to me it seems to die;
  To set glad lips against the lips of Death--
  The only thing God gives that comforteth,
The only thing we do not find a lie.

Spirit of
Dreams

I

Where hast thou folded thy pinions,
  Spirit of Dreams?
Hidden elusive garments
  Woven of gleams?
In what divine dominions,
  Brighter than day,
Far from the world's dark torments,
  Dost thou stay, dost thou stay?--
When shall my yearnings reach thee
  Again?
Not in vain let my soul beseech thee!
  Not in vain! not in vain!

II

I have longed for thee as a lover
  For her, the one;
As a brother for a sister
  Long dead and gone.
I have called thee over and over
  Names sweet to hear;
With words than music trister,
  And thrice as dear.

How long must my sad heart woo thee,
  Yet fail?
How long must my soul pursue thee,
  Nor avail, nor avail?

III

All night hath thy loving mother,
  Beautiful Sleep,
Lying beside me, listened
  And heard me weep.
But ever thou soughtest another
  Who sought thee not;
For him thy soft smile glistened--
  I was forgot.
When shall my soul behold thee
  As before?
When shall my heart infold thee?--
  Nevermore? nevermore?

LINES AND LYRICS

To a Wind-Flower

I

Teach me the secret of thy loveliness,
  That, being made wise, I may aspire to be
As beautiful in thought, and so express
  Immortal truths to earth's mortality;
Though to my soul ability be less
  Than 't is to thee, O sweet anemone.

II

Teach me the secret of thy innocence,
  That in simplicity I may grow wise;
Asking from Art no other recompense
  Than the approval of her own just eyes;
So may I rise to some fair eminence,
  Though less than thine, O cousin of the skies.

III

Teach me these things; through whose high knowledge, I,--
  When Death hath poured oblivion through my veins,
And brought me home, as all are brought, to lie
  In that vast house, common to serfs and Thanes,--
I shall not die, I shall not utterly die,
  For beauty born of beauty--***that*** remains.

Microcosm

The memory of what we've lost
Is with us more than what we've won;
Perhaps because we count the cost
By what we could, yet have not done.

'Twixt act and purpose fate hath drawn
Invisible threads we can not break,
And puppet-like these move us on
The stage of life, and break or make.

Less than the dust from which we're wrought,
We come and go, and still are hurled
From change to change, from naught to naught,
Heirs of oblivion and the world.

Fortune

Within the hollowed hand of God,
Blood-red they lie, the dice of fate,
That have no time nor period,
And know no early and no late.

Postpone you can not, nor advance
Success or failure that's to be;
All fortune, being born of chance,
Is bastard-child to destiny.

Bow down your head, or hold it high,
Consent, defy--no smallest part
Of this you change, although the die
Was fashioned from your living heart.

Death

Through some strange sense of sight or touch
I find what all have found before,
The presence I have feared so much,
The unknown's immaterial door.

I seek not and it comes to me:
I do not know the thing I find:

The fillet of fatality
Drops from my brows that made me blind.

Point forward now or backward, light!
The way I take I may not choose:
Out of the night into the night,
And in the night no certain clews.

But on the future, dim and vast,
And dark with dust and sacrifice,
Death's towering ruin from the past
Makes black the land that round me lies.

The
Soul

An heritage of hopes and fears
And dreams and memory,
And vices of ten thousand years
God gives to thee.

A house of clay, the home of Fate,
Haunted of Love and Sin,
Where Death stands knocking at the gate
To let him in.

Conscience

Within the soul are throned two powers,
One, Love; one, Hate. Begot of these,
And veiled between, a presence towers,
The shadowy keeper of the keys.

With wild command or calm persuasion
This one may argue, that compel;
Vain are concealment and evasion--
For each he opens heaven and hell.

Youth

I

Morn's mystic rose is reddening on the hills,
Dawn's irised nautilus makes glad the sea;
There is a lyre of flame that throbs and fills
Far heaven and earth with hope's wild ecstasy.--
    With lilied field and grove,
    Haunts of the turtle-dove,
      Here is the land of Love.

II

The chariot of the noon makes blind the blue
As towards the goal his burning axle glares;
There is a fiery trumpet thrilling through
Wide heaven and earth with deeds of one who dares.--
        With peaks of splendid name,
        Wrapped round with astral flame,
          Here is the land of Fame.

III

The purple priesthood of the evening waits
With golden pomp within the templed skies;
There is a harp of worship at the gates
Of heaven and earth that bids the soul arise.--
        With columned cliffs and long
        Vales, music breathes among,
          Here is the land of Song.

IV

Moon-crowned, the epic of the night unrolls
Its starry utterance o'er height and deep;
There is a voice of beauty at the souls
Of heaven and earth that lulls the heart asleep.--
        With storied woods and streams,
        Where marble glows and gleams,
          Here is the land of Dreams.

Life's
Seasons

I

When all the world was Mayday,
  And all the skies were blue,
Young innocence made playday
  Among the flowers and dew;
Then all of life was Mayday,
  And clouds were none or few.

II

When all the world was Summer,
  And morn shone overhead,
Love was the sweet newcomer
  Who led youth forth to wed;
Then all of life was Summer,
  And clouds were golden red.

III

When earth was all October,
  And days were gray with mist,
On woodways, sad and sober,

Grave memory kept her tryst;
Then life was all October,
  And clouds were twilight-kissed.

IV

Now all the world's December,
  And night is all alarm,
Above the last dim ember
  Grief bends to keep him warm;
Now all of life's December,
  And clouds are driven storm.

Old
Homes

Old homes among the hills! I love their gardens,
Their old rock-fences, that our day inherits;
Their doors, 'round which the great trees stand like wardens;
Their paths, down which the shadows march like spirits;
Broad doors and paths that reach bird-haunted gardens.

I see them gray among their ancient acres,
Severe of front, their gables lichen-sprinkled,--
Like gentle-hearted, solitary Quakers,
Grave and religious, with kind faces wrinkled,--
Serene among their memory-hallowed acres.

Their gardens, banked with roses and with lilies--
Those sweet aristocrats of all the flowers--
Where Springtime mints her gold in daffodillies,
And Autumn coins her marigolds in showers,
And all the hours are toilless as the lilies.

I love their orchards where the gay woodpecker
Flits, flashing o'er you, like a winged jewel;
Their woods, whose floors of moss the squirrels checker
With half-hulled nuts; and where, in cool renewal,
The wild brooks laugh, and raps the red woodpecker.

Old homes! old hearts! Upon my soul forever
Their peace and gladness lie like tears and laughter;
Like love they touch me, through the years that sever,
With simple faith; like friendship, draw me after
The dreamy patience that is theirs forever.

Field and
Forest Call

There is a field, that leans upon two hills,
Foamed o'er with flowers and twinkling with clear rills;
That in its girdle of wild acres bears
The anodyne of rest that cures all cares;
Wherein soft wind and sun and sound are blent
And fragrance--as in some old instrument
Sweet chords--calm things, that nature's magic spell

Distils from heaven's azure crucible,
And pours on Earth to make the sick mind well.
    There lies the path, they say--
    Come, away! come, away!

There is a forest, lying 'twixt two streams,
Sung through of birds and haunted of dim dreams;
That in its league-long hand of trunk and leaf
Lifts a green wand that charms away all grief;
Wrought of quaint silence and the stealth of things,
Vague, whispering touches, gleams and twitterings,
Dews and cool shadows--that the mystic soul
Of nature permeates with suave control,
And waves o'er earth to make the sad heart whole.
    There lies the road, they say--
    Come, away! come, away!

Meeting in Summer

    A tranquil bar
Of rosy twilight under dusk's first star.

    A glimmering sound
Of whispering waters over grassy ground.

    A sun-sweet smell
Of fresh-reaped hay from dewy field and dell.

A lazy breeze
Jostling the ripeness from the apple-trees.

A vibrant cry,
Passing, then gone, of bullbats in the sky.

And faintly now
The katydid upon the shadowy bough.

And far-off then
The little owl within the lonely glen.

And soon, full soon,
The silvery arrival of the moon.

And, to your door,
The path of roses I have trod before.

And, sweetheart, you!
Among the roses and the moonlit dew.

Swinging

Under the boughs of spring
She swung in the old rope-swing.

Her cheeks, with their happy blood,
Were pink as the apple-bud.

Her eyes, with their deep delight,
Were glad as the stars of night.

Her curls, with their romp and fun,
Were hoiden as wind and sun.

Her lips, with their laughter shrill,
Were wild as a woodland rill.

Under the boughs of spring
She swung in the old rope-swing.

And I,--who leaned on the fence,
Watching her innocence,

As, under the boughs that bent,
Now high, now low, she went,

In her soul the ecstasies
Of the stars, the brooks, the breeze,--

Had given the rest of my years,
With their blessings, and hopes, and fears,

To have been as she was then;
And, just for a moment, again

A boy in the old rope-swing
Under the boughs of spring.

Rosemary

Above her, pearl and rose the heavens lay;
Around her, flowers scattered earth with gold,
Or down the path in insolence held sway--
Like cavaliers who ride the elves' highway--
Scarlet and blue, within a garden old.

Beyond the hills, faint-heard through belts of wood,
Bells, Sabbath-sweet, swooned from some far-off town;
Gamboge and gold, broad sunset colors strewed
The purple west as if, with God imbued,
Her mighty pallet Nature there laid down.

Amid such flowers, underneath such skies,
Embodying all life knows of sweet and fair,
She stood; love's dreams in girlhood's face and eyes,
White as a star that comes to emphasize
The mingled beauty of the earth and air.

Behind her, seen through vines and orchard trees,
Gray with its twinkling windows--like the face
Of calm old-age that sits and smiles at ease--
Porched with old roses, haunts of honey-bees,
The homestead loomed dim in a glimmering space.

Ah! whom she waited in the afterglow,
Soft-eyed and dreamy 'mid the lily and rose,
I do not know, I do not wish to know;--
It is enough I keep her picture so,
Hung up, like poetry, o'er my life's dull prose.

A fragrant picture, where I still may find
Her face untouched of sorrow or regret,
Unspoiled of contact, ever young and kind,
Glad spiritual sweetheart of my soul and mind,
She had not been, perhaps, if we had met.

Ghost
Stories

When the hoot of the owl comes over the hill,
At twelve o'clock when the night is still,
And pale on the pools, where the creek-frogs croon,
Glimmering gray is the light o' the moon;
And under the willows, where waters lie,
The torch of the firefly wanders by;
They say that the miller walks here, walks here,
All covered with chaff, with his crooked staff,
And his horrible hobble and hideous laugh;
The old lame miller hung many a year:
When the hoot of the owl comes over the hill,
He walks alone by the rotting mill.

When the bark of the fox comes over the hill,
At twelve o'clock when the night is shrill,
And faint, on the ways where the crickets creep,
The starlight fails and the shadows sleep;
And under the willows, that toss and moan,
The glow-worm kindles its lanthorn lone;

They say that a woman floats dead, floats dead,
In a weedy space that the lilies lace,
A curse in her eyes and a smile on her face,
The miller's young wife with a gash in her head:
When the bark of the fox comes over the hill,
She floats alone by the rotting mill.

When the howl of the hound comes over the hill,
At twelve o'clock when the night is ill,
And the thunder mutters and forests sob,
And the fox-fire glows like the lamp of a Lob;
And under the willows, that gloom and glance,
The will-o'-the-wisps hold a devils' dance;
They say that that crime is re-acted again,
And each cranny and chink of the mill doth wink
With the light o' hell or the lightning's blink,
And a woman's shrieks come wild through the rain:
When the howl of the hound comes over the hill,
That murder returns to the rotting mill.

Dolce far Niente

I

Over the bay as our boat went sailing
  Under the skies of Augustine,
Far to the East lay the ocean paling
  Under the skies of Augustine.--
There, in the boat as we sat together,
Soft in the glow of the turquoise weather,
Light as the foam or a seagull's feather,
Fair of form and of face serene,
Sweet at my side I felt you lean,
As over the bay our boat went sailing
  Under the skies of Augustine.

II

Over the bay as our boat went sailing
  Under the skies of Augustine,
Pine and palm, to the West, hung, trailing
  Under the skies of Augustine.--
Was it the wind that sighed above you?
Was it the wave that whispered of you?
Was it my soul that said "I love you"?
Was it your heart that murmured between,
Answering, shy as a bird unseen?

As over the bay our boat went sailing
  Under the skies of Augustine.

III

Over the bay as our boat went sailing
  Under the skies of Augustine,
Gray and low flew the heron wailing
  Under the skies of Augustine.--
Naught was spoken. We watched the simple
Gulls wing past. Your hat's white wimple
Shadowed your eyes. And your lips, a-dimple,
Smiled and seemed from your soul to wean
An inner beauty, an added sheen,
As over the bay our boat went sailing
  Under the skies of Augustine.

IV

Over the bay as our boat went sailing
  Under the skies of Augustine,
Red on the marshes the day flared, failing
  Under the skies of Augustine.--
Was it your thought, or the transitory
Gold of the West, like a dreamy story,
Bright on your brow, that I read? the glory
And grace of love, like a rose-crowned queen
Pictured pensive in mind and mien?
As over the bay our boat went sailing

Under the skies of Augustine.

V

Over the bay as our boat went sailing
  Under the skies of Augustine,
Wan on the waters the mist lay veiling
  Under the skies of Augustine.--
Was it the joy that begot the sorrow?--
Joy that was filled with the dreams that borrow
Prescience sad of a far To-morrow,--
There in the Now that was all too keen,
That shadowed the fate that might intervene?
As over the bay our boat went sailing
  Under the skies of Augustine.

VI

Over the bay as our boat went sailing
  Under the skies of Augustine,
The marsh-hen cried and the tide was ailing
  Under the skies of Augustine.--
And so we parted. No vows were spoken.
No faith was plighted that might be broken.
But deep in our hearts each bore a token
Of life and of love and of all they mean,
Beautiful, thornless and ever green,
As over the bay our boat went sailing
  Under the skies of Augustine.

St. Augustine, Fla.

Words

I cannot tell what I would tell thee,
　What I would say, what thou shouldst hear:
Words of the soul that should compell thee,
　Words of the heart to draw thee near.

For when thou smilest, thou, who fillest
　My life with joy, and I would speak,
'T is then my lips and tongue are stillest,
　Knowing all language is too weak.

Look in my eyes: read there confession:
　The truest love has least of art:
Nor needs it words for its expression
　When soul speaks soul and heart speaks heart.

Reasons

I

Yea, why I love thee let my heart repeat:
  I look upon thy face and then divine
  How men could die for beauty, such as thine,--
      Deeming it sweet
To lay my life and manhood at thy feet,
  And for a word, a glance,
  Do deeds of old romance.

II

Yea, why I love thee let my heart unfold:
  I look into thy heart and then I know
  The wondrous poetry of the long-ago,
      The Age of Gold,
That speaks strange music, that is old, so old,
  Yet young, as when 't was born,
  With all the youth of morn.

III

Yea, why I love thee let my heart conclude:
  I look into thy soul and realize
  The undiscovered meaning of the skies,--

That long have wooed
The world with far ideals that elude,--
  Out of whose dreams, maybe,
  God shapes reality.

Evasion

Why do I love you, who have never given
  My heart encouragement or any cause?
Is it because, as earth is held of heaven,
  Your soul holds mine by some mysterious laws?
Perhaps, unseen of me, within your eyes
  The answer lies, the answer lies.

II

From your sweet lips no word hath ever fallen
  To tell my heart its love is not in vain--
The bee that wooes the flow'r hath honey and pollen
  To cheer him on and bring him back again:
But what have I, your other friends above,
  To feed my love, to feed my love?

III

Still, still you are my dream and my desire;
 Your love is an allurement and a dare
Set for attainment, like a shining spire,
 Far, far above me in the starry air:
And gazing upward, 'gainst the hope of hope,
 I breast the slope, I breast the slope.

In
May

I

When you and I in the hills went Maying,
 You and I in the sweet May weather,
 The birds, that sang on the boughs together,
There in the green of the woods, kept saying
 All that my heart was saying low,
 Love, as glad as the May's glad glow,--
   And did you know?
When you and I in the hills went Maying.

II

There where the brook on its rocks went winking,
  There by its banks where the May had led us,
  Flowers, that bloomed in the woods and meadows,
Azure and gold at our feet, kept thinking
  All that my soul was thinking there,
  Love, as pure as the May's pure air,--
      And did you care?
There where the brook on its rocks went winking.

III

Whatever befalls through fate's compelling,
  Should our paths unite or our pathways sever,
  In the Mays to come I shall feel forever
The wildflowers thinking, the wildbirds telling
  The same fond love that my heart then knew,
  Love unspeakable, deep and true,--
      But what of you?
Whatever befalls through fate's compelling.

Will You
Forget?

In years to come, will you forget,
Dear girl, how often we have met?
And I have gazed into your eyes
And there beheld no sad regret
To cloud the gladness of their skies,
While in your heart--unheard as yet--
Love slept, oblivious of my sighs?--
In years to come, will you forget?

Ah, me! I only pray that when,
In other days, some man of men
Has taught those eyes to laugh and weep
With joy and sorrow, hearts must ken
When love awakens in their deep,--
I only pray some memory then,
Or sad or sweet, you still will keep
Of me and love that might have been.

Clouds of the
Autumn Night

Clouds of the autumn night,
  Under the hunter's moon,--
Ghostly and windy white,--
  Whither, like leaves wild strewn,
Take ye your stormy flight?

Out of the west, where dusk,
  From her rich windowsill,
Leaned with a wand of tusk,
  Witch-like, and wood and hill
Phantomed with mist and musk.

Into the east, where morn
  Sleeps in a shadowy close,
Shut with a gate of horn,
  'Round which the dreams she knows
Flutter with rose and thorn.

Blow from the west, oh, blow,
  Clouds that the tempest steers!
And with your rain and snow
  Bear of my heart the tears,
And of my soul the woe.

Into the east then pass,
  Clouds that the night winds sweep!
And on her grave's sear grass,

There where she lies asleep.
There let them fall, alas!

The Glory
and the Dream

There in the past I see her as of old,
Blue-eyed and hazel-haired, within a room
Dim with a twilight of tenebrious gold;
Her white face sensuous as a delicate bloom
Night opens in the tropics. Fold on fold
Pale laces drape her; and a frail perfume,
As of a moonlit primrose brimmed with rain,
Breathes from her presence, drowsing heart and brain.

Her head is bent; some red carnations glow
Deep in her heavy hair; her large eyes gleam;--
Bright sister stars of those twin worlds of snow,
Her breasts, through which the veined violets stream;--
I hold her hand; her smile comes sweetly slow
As thoughts of love that haunt a poet's dream;
And at her feet once more I sit and hear
Wild words of passion--dead this many a year.

Snow
and Fire

Deep-hearted roses of the purple dusk
And lilies of the morn;
And cactus, holding up a slender tusk
Of fragrance on a thorn;
All heavy flowers, sultry with their musk,
Her presence puts to scorn.

For she is like the pale, pale snowdrop there,
Scentless and chaste of heart;
The moonflower, making spiritual the air,
Like some pure work of art;
Divine and holy, exquisitely fair,
And virtue's counterpart.

Yet when her eyes gaze into mine, and when
Her lips to mine are pressed,--
Why are my veins all fire then? and then
Why should her soul suggest
Voluptuous perfumes, maddening unto men,
And prurient with unrest?

Restraint

Dear heart and love! what happiness to sit
And watch the firelight's varying shade and shine
On thy young face; and through those eyes of thine--
As through glad windows--mark fair fancies flit
In sumptuous chambers of thy soul's chaste wit
Like graceful women: then to take in mine
Thy hand, whose pressure brims my heart's divine
Hushed rapture as with music exquisite!
When I remember how thy look and touch
Sway, like the moon, my blood with ecstasy,
I dare not think to what fierce heaven might lead
Thy soft embrace; or in thy kiss how much
Sweet hell,--beyond all help of me,--might be,
Where I were lost, where I were lost indeed!

Why Should
I Pine?

Why should I pine? when there in Spain
Are eyes to woo, and not in vain;
Dark eyes, and dreamily divine:
And lips, as red as sunlit wine;

Sweet lips, that never know disdain:

And hearts, for passion over fain;
Fond, trusting hearts that know no stain
  Of scorn for hearts that love like mine.--
    Why should I pine?

Because all dreams I entertain
Of beauty wear thy form, Elain;
  And e'en their lips and eyes are thine:
  So though I gladly would resign
All love, I love, and still complain,
    "Why should I pine?"

When Lydia Smiles

When Lydia smiles, I seem to see
The walls around me fade and flee;
  And, lo, in haunts of hart and hind
  I seem with lovely Rosalind,
In Arden 'neath the greenwood tree:
The day is drowsy with the bee,
And one wild bird flutes dreamily,
  And all the mellow air is kind,
    When Lydia smiles.

Ah, me! what were this world to me
Without her smile!--What poetry,
  What glad hesperian paths I find

Of love, that lead my soul and mind
To happy hills of Arcady,
     When Lydia smiles!

The
Rose

You have forgot: it once was red
With life, this rose, to which you said,--
  When, there in happy days gone by,
  You plucked it, on my breast to lie,--
"Sleep there, O rose! how sweet a bed
Is thine!--And, heart, be comforted;
For, though we part and roses shed
  Their leaves and fade, love cannot die.--"
     You have forgot.

So by those words of yours I'm led
To send it you this day you wed.
  Look well upon it. You, as I,
  Should ask it now, without a sigh,
If love can lie as it lies dead.--
     You have forgot.

A Ballad
of Sweethearts

Summer may come, in sun-blonde splendor,
To reap the harvest that Springtime sows;
And Fall lead in her old defender,
  Winter, all huddled up in snows:
  Ever a-south the love-wind blows
Into my heart, like a vane asway
  From face to face of the girls it knows--
But who is the fairest it's hard to say.

If Carrie smile or Maud look tender,
  Straight in my bosom the gladness glows;
But scarce at their side am I all surrender
  When Gertrude sings where the garden grows:
  And my heart is a bloom, like the red rose shows
For her hand to gather and toss away,
  Or wear on her breast, as her fancy goes--
But who is the fairest it's hard to say.

Let Laura pass, as a sapling slender,
  Her cheek a berry, her mouth a rose,--
Or Blanche or Helen,--to each I render
  The worship due to the charms she shows:
  But Mary's a poem when these are prose;
Here at her feet my life I lay;
  All of devotion to her it owes--
But who is the fairest it's hard to say.

How *can* my heart of my hand dispose?
  When Ruth and Clara, and Kate and May,
In form and feature no flaw disclose--
  But who is the fairest it's hard to say.

Her
Portrait

Were I an artist, Lydia, I
  Would paint you as you merit,
Not as my eyes, but dreams, descry;
  Not in the flesh, but spirit.

The canvas I would paint you on
  Should be a bit of heaven;
My brush, a sunbeam; pigments, dawn
  And night and starry even.

Your form and features to express,
  Likewise your soul's chaste whiteness,
I'd take the primal essences
  Of darkness and of brightness.

I'd take pure night to paint your hair;
  Stars for your eyes; and morning
To paint your skin--the rosy air
  That is your limbs' adorning.

To paint the love-bows of your lips,
  I'd mix, for colors, kisses;
And for your breasts and finger-tips,
  Sweet odors and soft blisses.

And to complete the picture well,
  I'd temper all with woman,--
Some tears, some laughter; heaven and hell,
  To show you still are human.

A Song
for Yule

I

Sing, Hey, when the time rolls round this way,
And the bells peal out, *'Tis Christmas Day*;
The world is better then by half,
    For joy, for joy;
In a little while you will see it laugh--
For a song's to sing and a glass to quaff,
    My boy, my boy.
So here's to the man who never says nay!--
Sing, Hey, a song of Christmas-Day!

II

Sing, Ho, when roofs are white with snow,
And homes are hung with mistletoe;
Old Earth is not half bad, I wis--
    What cheer! what cheer!
How it ever seemed sad the wonder is--
With a gift to give and a girl to kiss,
    My dear, my dear.
So here's to the girl who never says no!
Sing, Ho, a song of the mistletoe!

III

No thing in the world to the heart seems wrong
When the soul of a man walks out with song;
Wherever they go, glad hand in hand,
    And glove in glove,
The round of the land is rainbow-spanned,
And the meaning of life they understand
    Is love, is love.
Let the heart be open, the soul be strong,
And life will be glad as a Christmas song.

The Puritans'
Christmas

Their only thought religion,
  What Christmas joys had they,
The stern, staunch Pilgrim Fathers who
  Knew naught of holiday?--

A log-church in the clearing
  'Mid solitudes of snow,
The wild-beast and the wilderness,
  And lurking Indian foe.

No time had they for pleasure,
  Whom God had put to school;
A sermon was their Christmas cheer,
  A psalm their only Yule.

They deemed it joy sufficient,--
  Nor would Christ take it ill,--
That service to Himself and God
  Employed their spirits still.

And so through faith and prayer
  Their powers were renewed,
And souls made strong to shape a World,
  And tame a solitude.

A type of revolution,
  Wrought from an iron plan,

In the largest mold of liberty
 God cast the Puritan.

A better land they founded,
 That Freedom had for bride,
The shackles of old despotism
 Struck from her limbs and side.

With faith within to guide them,
 And courage to perform,
A nation, from a wilderness,
 They hewed with their strong arm.

For liberty to worship,
 And right to do and dare,
They faced the savage and the storm
 With voices raised in prayer.

For God it was who summoned,
 And God it was who led,
And God would not forsake the love
 That must be clothed and fed.

Great need had they of courage!
 Great need of faith had they!
And lacking these--how otherwise
 For us had been this day!

Spring

(After the German of Goethe, *Faust*, II)

When on the mountain tops ray-crowned Apollo
Turns his swift arrows, dart on glittering dart,
Let but a rock glint green, the wild goats follow
Glad-grazing shyly on each sparse-grown part.

Rolled into plunging torrents spring the fountains;
And slope and vale and meadowland grow green;
While on ridg'd levels of a hundred mountains,
Far fleece by fleece, the woolly flocks convene.

With measured stride, deliberate and steady,
The scattered cattle seek the beetling steep,
But shelter for th' assembled herd is ready
In many hollows that the walled rocks heap:

The lairs of Pan; and, lo, in murmuring places,
In bushy clefts, what woodland Nymphs arouse!
Where, full of yearning for the azure spaces,
Tree, crowding tree, lifts high its heavy boughs.

Old forests, where the gnarly oak stands regnant
Bristling with twigs that still repullulate,
And, swoln with spring, with sappy sweetness pregnant,
The maple blushes with its leafy weight.

And, mother-like, in cirques of quiet shadows,
Milk flows, warm milk, that keeps all things alive;

Fruit is not far, th' abundance of the meadows,
And honey oozes from the hollow hive.

Lines

Within the world of every man's desire
Three things have power to lift his soul above,
Through dreams, religion, and ecstatic fire,
The star-like shapes of Beauty, Truth, and Love.

I never hoped that, this side far-off Heaven,
These three,--whom all exalted souls pursue,--
I e'er should see; until to me 't was given,
Lady, to meet the three, made one, in you.

When Ships put out to Sea

I

It's "Sweet, good-bye," when pennants fly
  And ships put out to sea;
It's a loving kiss, and a tear or two
In an eye of brown or an eye of blue;--
  And you'll remember me,

Sweetheart,
And you'll remember me.

II

It's "Friend or foe?" when signals blow
  And ships sight ships at sea;
It's clear for action, and man the guns,
As the battle nears or the battle runs;--
  And you'll remember me,
    Sweetheart,
  And you'll remember me.

III

It's deck to deck, and wrath and wreck
  When ships meet ships at sea;
It's scream of shot and shriek of shell,
And hull and turret a roaring hell;--
  And you'll remember me,
    Sweetheart,
  And you'll remember me.

IV

It's doom and death, and pause a breath
  When ships go down at sea;
It's hate is over and love begins,
And war is cruel whoever wins;--
  And you'll remember me,

Sweetheart,
And you'll remember me.

The
"Kentucky"

(Battleship, launched March 24, 1898.)

I

Here's to her who bears the name
   Of our State;
May the glory of her fame
   Be as great!
In the battle's dread eclipse,
When she opens iron lips,
When our ships confront the ships
   Of the foe,
May each word of steel she utters carry woe!
   Here's to her!

II

Here's to her, who, like a knight
   Mailed of old,
From far sea to sea the Right

Shall uphold.
May she always deal defeat,--
When contending navies meet,
And the battle's screaming sleet
   Blinds and stuns,--
With the red, terrific thunder of her guns.
   Here's to her!

III

Here's to her who bears the name
   Of our State;
May the glory of her fame
   Be as great!
Like a beacon, like a star,
May she lead our squadrons far,--
When the hurricane of war
   Shakes the world,--
With her pennant in the vanward broad unfurled.
   Here's to her!

Quatrains

I

MOTHS AND FIREFLIES

Since Fancy taught me in her school of spells
I know her tricks--These are not moths at all,
Nor fireflies; but masking Elfland belles
Whose link-boys torch them to Titania's ball.

II

AUTUMN WILD-FLOWERS

Like colored lanterns swung in Elfin towers,
Wild morning-glories light the tangled ways,
And, like the rosy rockets of the Fays,
Burns the sloped crimson of the cardinal-flowers.

III

THE WIND IN THE PINES

When winds go organing through the pines
On hill and headland, darkly gleaming,
Meseems I hear sonorous lines

Of Iliads that the woods are dreaming.

IV

OPPORTUNITY

Behold a hag whom Life denies a kiss
As he rides questward in knighterrant-wise;
Only when he hath passed her is it his
To know, too late, the Fairy in disguise.

V

DREAMS

They mock the present and they haunt the past,
And in the future there is naught agleam
With hope, the soul desires, that at last
The heart pursuing does not find a dream.

VI

THE STARS

These--the bright symbols of man's hope and fame,
In which he reads his blessing or his curse--
Are syllables with which God speaks His name

In the vast utterance of the universe.

VII

BEAUTY

High as a star, yet lowly as a flower,
Unknown she takes her unassuming place
At Earth's proud masquerade--the appointed hour
Strikes, and, behold, the marvel of her face.

Processional

Universes are the pages
Of that book whose words are ages;
Of that book which destiny
Opens in eternity.

There each syllable expresses
Silence; there each thought a guess is;
In whose rhetoric's cosmic runes
Roll the worlds and swarming moons.

There the systems, we call solar,
Equatorial and polar,
Write their lines of rushing light
On the awful leaves of night.

There the comets, vast and streaming,
Punctuate the heavens' gleaming
Scroll; and suns, gigantic, shine,
Periods to each starry line.

There, initials huge, the Lion
Looms and measureless Orion;
And, as 'neath a chapter done,
Burns the Great-Bear's colophon.

Constellated, hieroglyphic,
Numbering each page terrific,
Fiery on the nebular black,
Flames the hurling zodiac.

In that book, o'er which Chaldean
Wisdom pored and many an eon
Of philosophy long dead,
This is all that man has read:--

He has read how good and evil,--
In creation's wild upheaval,--
Warred; while God wrought terrible
At foundations red of Hell.

He has read of man and woman;
Laws and gods, both beast and human;
Thrones of hate and creeds of lust,
Vanished now and turned to dust.

Arts and manners that have crumbled;
Cities buried; empires tumbled:
Time but breathed on them its breath;

Earth is builded of their death.

These but lived their little hour,
Filled with pride and pomp and power;
What availed them all at last?
We shall pass as they have past.

Still the human heart will dream on
Love, part angel and part demon;
Yet, I question, what secures
Our belief that aught endures?

In that book, o'er which Chaldean
Wisdom pored and many an eon
Of philosophy long dead,
This is all that man has read.

SOME NOTICES OF MR. CAWEIN'S VERSES

"I should like to praise the poetry of Madison Cawein, of Kentucky, which is as remote as Greece from the actual everyday life of his region; as remote from it as the poetry of Keats was from the England of his day, and which is yet so richly, so passionately true to the presence and essence of nature as she can be known only in the Southern West. I named Keats with no purpose of likening this young poet to him, but since he is named it is impossible not to recognize that they are of the same Hellenic race; full of like rapture in sky and field and stream, and of a like sensitive reluctance from whatever chills the joy of sense in youth, in love, in melancholy. I know Mr. Cawein has faults, and very probably he knows it, too; his delight in color sometimes plunges him into mere paint; his wish to follow a subtle thought or emotion sometimes lures him into empty dusks; his devotion to nature sometimes contents him with solitudes bereft of the human interest by which alone the landscape lives. But he is, to my thinking, a most genuine poet, and one of these few Americans, who, even in their over-refinement, could never be mistaken for Europeans; who perhaps by reason of it are only the more American."--WILLIAM DEAN HOWELLS in *Literature*.

"From the poetry of our day I select that of Madison Cawein as an example of conspicuous merit. Many American readers have enjoyed Mr. Cawein's productions.... But the appreciation of his poetry has never been as great as its merits would indicate. His poems are rather too good to be caught up on the babbling tongue and cast forth into mere popularity. They are caviare to the general; and yet they have in them the best elements of popular favor.

"Cawein is a classicist. He will have it that poems, however humble the theme, however tender the sentiment, shall wear a tasteful Attic dress. I do not intimate that Mr. Cawein's mind has been too much saturated with the classical spirit or that his native instincts have been supplanted with Greek exotics and flowers out of the renaissance, but rather that his own mental constitution is of a classical as well as a romantic mould.

"The themes of Cawein's poetry are generally taken from the world of romance. If there be any modern bard who can recreate a mediaeval castle and give to its inhabitants the sentiments which were theirs in the twelfth century, Cawein is the poet who can. He takes delight in the East. He is the Omar Khayyam of the Ohio Valley. He is as much of a Mohammedan as a Christian. He knows the son of Abdallah better than he knows Cromwell; and has more sympathy with a Khalif than with a Colonel. He dwells in the romantic regions of life; but the romance is real. The hope is a true hope. The dream is a true dream. The picture is a painting, and not a chromo. The love is a passion, and not a dilettante episode. Cawein's art is a genuine art. His verse is exquisite. Out of the three hundred and thirteen poems in the five volumes under consideration there may be found hardly a false or broken harmony...."--JOHN CLARK RIDPATH, LL.D., in The Arena.

"The rattlesnake-weed and the bluet-bloom were unknown to Herrick and to Wordsworth, but such art as Mr. Cawein's makes them at home in English poetry. There is passion, too, and thought in his equipment...."--WILLIAM ARCHER in the *Pall Mall Magazine*.

"I find in the best pieces an intoxicating sense of beauty, a richness, that is rarely achieved, although every young poet nowadays strives after it. I find, too, a daring use of language which sometimes, nay often, conducts to genuine and startling felicities."--EDMUND GOSSE.

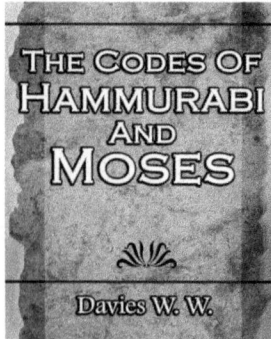

The Codes Of Hammurabi And Moses
W. W. Davies

QTY

The discovery of the Hammurabi Code is one of the greatest achievements of archaeology, and is of paramount interest, not only to the student of the Bible, but also to all those interested in ancient history...

Religion   ISBN: *1-59462-338-4*   Pages:132
MSRP $12.95

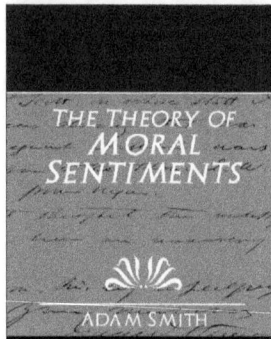

The Theory of Moral Sentiments
Adam Smith

QTY

This work from 1749. contains original theories of conscience amd moral judgment and it is the foundation for systemof morals.

Philosophy ISBN: *1-59462-777-0*   Pages:536
MSRP $19.95

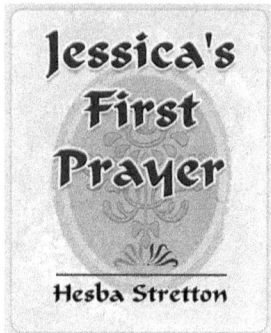

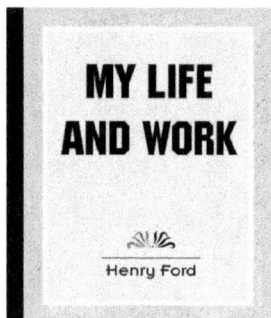

Jessica's First Prayer
Hesba Stretton

QTY

In a screened and secluded corner of one of the many railway-bridges which span the streets of London there could be seen a few years ago, from five o'clock every morning until half past eight, a tidily set-out coffee-stall, consisting of a trestle and board, upon which stood two large tin cans, with a small fire of charcoal burning under each so as to keep the coffee boiling during the early hours of the morning when the work-people were thronging into the city on their way to their daily toil...

Pages:84

Childrens   ISBN: *1-59462-373-2*   *MSRP $9.95*

My Life and Work
Henry Ford

QTY

Henry Ford revolutionized the world with his implementation of mass production for the Model T automobile. Gain valuable business insight into his life and work with his own auto-biography... "We have only started on our development of our country we have not as yet, with all our talk of wonderful progress, done more than scratch the surface. The progress has been wonderful enough but..."

Pages:300

Biographies/   ISBN: *1-59462-198-5*   *MSRP $21.95*

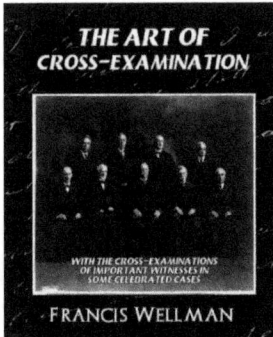

The Art of Cross-Examination
Francis Wellman

QTY

I presume it is the experience of every author, after his first book is published upon an important subject, to be almost overwhelmed with a wealth of ideas and illustrations which could readily have been included in his book, and which to his own mind, at least, seem to make a second edition inevitable. Such certainly was the case with me; and when the first edition had reached its sixth impression in five months, I rejoiced to learn that it seemed to my publishers that the book had met with a sufficiently favorable reception to justify a second and considerably enlarged edition. ..

Pages:412

Reference   ISBN: *1-59462-647-2*   *MSRP $19.95*

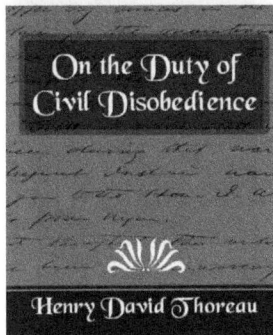

On the Duty of Civil Disobedience
Henry David Thoreau

QTY

Thoreau wrote his famous essay, On the Duty of Civil Disobedience, as a protest against an unjust but popular war and the immoral but popular institution of slave-owning. He did more than write—he declined to pay his taxes, and was hauled off to gaol in consequence. Who can say how much this refusal of his hastened the end of the war and of slavery ?

Law   ISBN: *1-59462-747-9*   **Pages:48**

MSRP $7.45

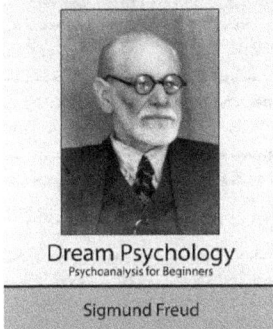

Dream Psychology Psychoanalysis for Beginners
Sigmund Freud

QTY

Sigmund Freud, born Sigismund Schlomo Freud (May 6, 1856 - September 23, 1939), was a Jewish-Austrian neurologist and psychiatrist who co-founded the psychoanalytic school of psychology. Freud is best known for his theories of the unconscious mind, especially involving the mechanism of repression; his redefinition of sexual desire as mobile and directed towards a wide variety of objects; and his therapeutic techniques, especially his understanding of transference in the therapeutic relationship and the presumed value of dreams as sources of insight into unconscious desires.

Pages:196

Psychology   ISBN: *1-59462-905-6*   *MSRP $15.45*

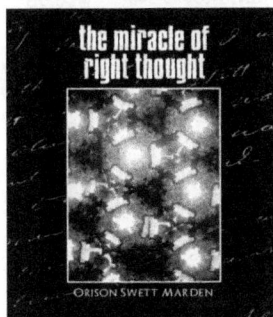

The Miracle of Right Thought
Orison Swett Marden

QTY

Believe with all of your heart that you will do what you were made to do. When the mind has once formed the habit of holding cheerful, happy, prosperous pictures, it will not be easy to form the opposite habit. It does not matter how improbable or how far away this realization may see, or how dark the prospects may be, if we visualize them as best we can, as vividly as possible, hold tenaciously to them and vigorously struggle to attain them, they will gradually become actualized, realized in the life. But a desire, a longing without endeavor, a yearning abandoned or held indifferently will vanish without realization.

Pages:360

Self Help   ISBN: *1-59462-644-8*   *MSRP $25.45*

The Rosicrucian Cosmo-Conception Mystic Christianity by *Max Heindel* ISBN: *1-59462-188-8* **$38.95**
The Rosicrucian Cosmo-conception is not dogmatic, neither does it appeal to any other authority than the reason of the student. It is: not controversial, but is: sent forth in the, hope that it may help to clear... New Age/Religion Pages 646

Abandonment To Divine Providence by *Jean-Pierre de Caussade* ISBN: *1-59462-228-0* **$25.95**
"The Rev. Jean Pierre de Caussade was one of the most remarkable spiritual writers of the Society of Jesus in France in the 18th Century. His death took place at Toulouse in 1751. His works have gone through many editions and have been republished... Inspirational/Religion Pages 400

Mental Chemistry by *Charles Haanel* ISBN: *1-59462-192-6* **$23.95**
Mental Chemistry allows the change of material conditions by combining and appropriately utilizing the power of the mind. Much like applied chemistry creates something new and unique out of careful combinations of chemicals the mastery of mental chemistry... New Age Pages 354

The Letters of Robert Browning and Elizabeth Barret Barrett 1845-1846 vol II ISBN: *1-59462-193-4* **$35.95**
by *Robert Browning* and *Elizabeth Barrett* Biographies Pages 596

Gleanings In Genesis (volume I) by *Arthur W. Pink* ISBN: *1-59462-130-6* **$27.45**
Appropriately has Genesis been termed "the seed plot of the Bible" for in it we have, in germ form, almost all of the great doctrines which are afterwards fully developed in the books of Scripture which follow... Religion/Inspirational Pages 420

The Master Key by *L. W. de Laurence* ISBN: *1-59462-001-6* **$30.95**
In no branch of human knowledge has there been a more lively increase of the spirit of research during the past few years than in the study of Psychology, Concentration and Mental Discipline. The requests for authentic lessons in Thought Control, Mental Discipline and... New Age/Business Pages 422

The Lesser Key Of Solomon Goetia by *L. W. de Laurence* ISBN: *1-59462-092-X* **$9.95**
This translation of the first book of the "Lernegton" which is now for the first time made accessible to students of Talismanic Magic was done, after careful collation and edition, from numerous Ancient Manuscripts in Hebrew, Latin, and French... New Age/Occult Pages 92

Rubaiyat Of Omar Khayyam by *Edward Fitzgerald* ISBN:*1-59462-332-5* **$13.95**
Edward Fitzgerald, whom the world has already learned, in spite of his own efforts to remain within the shadow of anonymity, to look upon as one of the rarest poets of the century, was born at Bredfield, in Suffolk, on the 31st of March, 1809. He was the third son of John Purcell... Music Pages 172

Ancient Law by *Henry Maine* ISBN: *1-59462-128-4* **$29.95**
The chief object of the following pages is to indicate some of the earliest ideas of mankind, as they are reflected in Ancient Law, and to point out the relation of those ideas to modern thought. Religion/History Pages 452

Far-Away Stories by *William J. Locke* ISBN: *1-59462-129-2* **$19.45**
"Good wine needs no bush, but a collection of mixed vintages does. And this book is just such a collection. Some of the stories I do not want to remain buried for ever in the museum files of dead magazine-numbers an author's not unpardonable vanity..." Fiction Pages 272

Life of David Crockett by *David Crockett* ISBN: *1-59462-250-7* **$27.45**
"Colonel David Crockett was one of the most remarkable men of the times in which he lived. Born in humble life, but gifted with a strong will, an indomitable courage, and unremitting perseverance... Biographies/New Age Pages 424

Lip-Reading by *Edward Nitchie* ISBN: *1-59462-206-X* **$25.95**
Edward B. Nitchie, founder of the New York School for the Hard of Hearing, now the Nitchie School of Lip-Reading, Inc, wrote "LIP-READING Principles and Practice". The development and perfecting of this meritorious work on lip-reading was an undertaking... How-to Pages 400

A Handbook of Suggestive Therapeutics, Applied Hypnotism, Psychic Science ISBN: *1-59462-214-0* **$24.95**
by *Henry Munro* Health/New Age/Health/Self-help Pages 376

A Doll's House: and Two Other Plays by *Henrik Ibsen* ISBN: *1-59462-112-8* **$19.95**
Henrik Ibsen created this classic when in revolutionary 1848 Rome. Introducing some striking concepts in playwriting for the realist genre, this play has been studied the world over. Fiction/Classics/Plays 308

The Light of Asia by *sir Edwin Arnold* ISBN: *1-59462-204-3* **$13.95**
In this poetic masterpiece, Edwin Arnold describes the life and teachings of Buddha. The man who was to become known as Buddha to the world was born as Prince Gautama of India but he rejected the worldly riches and abandoned the reigns of power when... Religion/History/Biographies Pages 170

The Complete Works of Guy de Maupassant by *Guy de Maupassant* ISBN: *1-59462-157-8* **$16.95**
"For days and days, nights and nights, I had dreamed of that first kiss which was to consecrate our engagement, and I knew not on what spot I should put my lips..." Fiction/Classics Pages 240

The Art of Cross-Examination by *Francis L. Wellman* ISBN: *1-59462-309-0* **$26.95**
Written by a renowned trial lawyer, Wellman imparts his experience and uses case studies to explain how to use psychology to extract desired information through questioning. How-to/Science/Reference Pages 408

Answered or Unanswered? by *Louisa Vaughan* ISBN: *1-59462-248-5* **$10.95**
Miracles of Faith in China Religion Pages 112

The Edinburgh Lectures on Mental Science (1909) by *Thomas* ISBN: *1-59462-008-3* **$11.95**
This book contains the substance of a course of lectures recently given by the writer in the Queen Street Hall, Edinburgh. Its purpose is to indicate the Natural Principles governing the relation between Mental Action and Material Conditions... New Age/Psychology Pages 148

Ayesha by *H. Rider Haggard* ISBN: *1-59462-301-5* **$24.95**
Verily and indeed it is the unexpected that happens! Probably if there was one person upon the earth from whom the Editor of this, and of a certain previous history, did not expect to hear again... Classics Pages 380

Ayala's Angel by *Anthony Trollope* ISBN: *1-59462-352-X* **$29.95**
The two girls were both pretty, but Lucy who was twenty-one who supposed to be simple and comparatively unattractive, whereas Ayala was credited, as her Bombwhat romantic name might show, with poetic charm and a taste for romance. Ayala when her father died was nineteen... Fiction Pages 484

The American Commonwealth by *James Bryce* ISBN: *1-59462-286-8* **$34.45**
An interpretation of American democratic political theory. It examines political mechanics and society from the perspective of Scotsman James Bryce Politics Pages 572

Stories of the Pilgrims by *Margaret P. Pumphrey* ISBN: *1-59462-116-0* **$17.95**
This book explores pilgrims religious oppression in England as well as their escape to Holland and eventual crossing to America on the Mayflower, and their early days in New England... History Pages 268

www.bookjungle.com *email: sales@bookjungle.com fax: 630-214-0564 mail: Book Jungle PO Box 2226 Champaign, IL 61825*

QTY

The Fasting Cure *by Sinclair Upton*   ISBN: *1-59462-222-1* $13.95
In the Cosmopolitan Magazine for May, 1910, and in the Contemporary Review (London) for April, 1910, I published an article dealing with my experiences in fasting. I have written a great many magazine articles, but never one which attracted so much attention... New Age/Self Help/Health Pages 164

Hebrew Astrology *by Sepharial*   ISBN: *1-59462-308-2* $13.45
In these days of advanced thinking it is a matter of common observation that we have left many of the old landmarks behind and that we are now pressing forward to greater heights and to a wider horizon than that which represented the mind-content of our progenitors... Astrology Pages 144

Thought Vibration or The Law of Attraction in the Thought World   ISBN: *1-59462-127-6* $12.95

by William Walker Atkinson   *Psychology/Religion Pages 144*

Optimism *by Helen Keller*   ISBN: *1-59462-108-X* $15.95
Helen Keller was blind, deaf, and mute since 19 months old, yet famously learned how to overcome these handicaps, communicate with the world, and spread her lectures promoting optimism. An inspiring read for everyone... Biographies/Inspirational Pages 84

Sara Crewe *by Frances Burnett*   ISBN: *1-59462-360-0* $9.45
In the first place, Miss Minchin lived in London. Her home was a large, dull, tall one, in a large, dull square, where all the houses were alike, and all the sparrows were alike, and where all the door-knockers made the same heavy sound... Childrens/Classic Pages 88

The Autobiography of Benjamin Franklin *by Benjamin Franklin*   ISBN: *1-59462-135-7* $24.95
The Autobiography of Benjamin Franklin has probably been more extensively read than any other American historical work, and no other book of its kind has had such ups and downs of fortune. Franklin lived for many years in England, where he was agent... Biographies/History Pages 332

Name	
Email	
Telephone	
Address	
City, State ZIP	

☐ **Credit Card**   ☐ **Check / Money Order**

Credit Card Number	
Expiration Date	
Signature	

Please Mail to: Book Jungle
                           PO Box 2226
                           Champaign, IL 61825
or Fax to: 630-214-0564

ORDERING INFORMATION

web: *www.bookjungle.com*
email: *sales@bookjungle.com*
fax: *630-214-0564*
mail: *Book Jungle PO Box 2226 Champaign, IL 61825*
or PayPal *to sales@bookjungle.com*

Please contact us for bulk discounts

DIRECT-ORDER TERMS

**20% Discount if You Order
Two or More Books**
Free Domestic Shipping!
Accepted: Master Card, Visa,
Discover, American Express